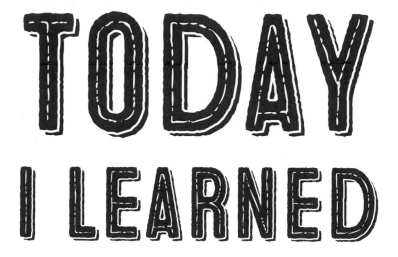

TODAY
I LEARNED

Published by Willow Creek Press, Inc.
P.O. Box 147, Minocqua, Wisconsin 54548

Printed in the United States

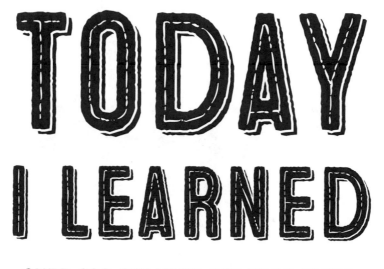

TODAY
I LEARNED

OVER 300 STRANGE-BUT-TRUE FACTS
THAT YOU PROBABLY DIDN'T KNOW.

☲ WILLOW CREEK PRESS®

THE STATUE OF LIBERTY USED TO BE A LIGHTHOUSE.

The Statue of Liberty is technically a lighthouse, and was at one point under the operation of the Lighthouse Board. However, it never properly functioned as a lighthouse.

THE UNICORN IS THE NATIONAL ANIMAL OF SCOTLAND.

In Celtic mythology the unicorn was a symbol of purity and innocence, as well as masculinity and power. Tales of dominance and chivalry associated with the unicorn may be why it was chosen as Scotland's national animal.

A GROUP OF CROWS IS CALLED A MURDER.

QUEEN ELIZABETH II IS A TRAINED MECHANIC.

AVOCADOS ARE A FRUIT, NOT A VEGETABLE.

A DIME HAS 118 RIDGES ON ITS EDGES.

CHAMPAGNE WAS ONCE USED AS A SHOE POLISH.

5

IT'S ILLEGAL TO OWN ONLY ONE GUINEA PIG IN SWITZERLAND.

Guinea pigs are social creatures who need interaction with their species in order to be happy, so the European country has made it illegal to own just one and considers it to be animal abuse.

ALL THE CLOCKS IN PULP FICTION ARE SET TO 4:20.

PSYCHO WAS THE FIRST MOVIE TO SHOW A TOILET FLUSHING.

COWS KILL MORE AMERICANS EACH YEAR THAN SHARKS DO.

PENNSYLVANIA IS MISSPELLED ON THE LIBERTY BELL.

On the Liberty Bell, Pennsylvania is misspelled "Pensylvania." This spelling was one of several acceptable spellings of the name at that time.

ONE SINGLE TEASPOON OF HONEY REPRESENTS THE LIFE WORK OF 12 BEES.

THE EIFFEL TOWER CAN BE 15 CM. TALLER DURING THE SUMMER.

This is a natural physical phenomenon called thermal expansion. Heat causes an increase in volume that makes the Eiffel Tower a few centimeters taller. This expansion also causes the Tower to tilt slightly away from the sun.

THERE IS A BEER PIPELINE IN GERMANY.

Bars in Gelsenkirchen, Germany have access to an underground pipeline filled with delicious, refreshing beer. The pipeline stretches over five kilometers and delivers over 14 liters of beer per minute. The beer originates from four cooling centers underneath the city's famous Veltins-Arena.

THE FIRST PERSON CONVICTED OF SPEEDING WAS GOING EIGHT MPH.

THE SHORTEST WAR IN HISTORY LASTED FOR ONLY 38 MINUTES.

FOR 20 YEARS, A CAT SERVED AS MAYOR OF AN ALASKAN TOWN.

BABY SEA OTTERS ARE UNABLE TO SWIM.

PHEASANT ISLAND IS GOVERNED BY SPAIN AND FRANCE.

The island is a condominium established by the Treaty of the Pyrenees in 1659, under joint sovereignty of Spain and France, and for alternating periods of six months is officially under the governance of the naval commanders of San Sebastián, Spain and of Bayonne, France.

THE SNOW IN THE WIZARD OF OZ IS ACTUALLY ASBESTOS.

BUBBLE WRAP WAS ORIGINALLY INTENDED TO BE WALLPAPER.

Bubble wrap was invented in 1957 by Alfred Fielding and Marc Chavannes as a textured wallpaper. To make the wallpaper, they sealed two shower curtains together, making sure that air bubbles were captured.

A JOCKEY FROM 1923 MANAGED TO FINISH A RACE AFTER DYING.

THE SPANISH NATIONAL ANTHEM HAS NO WORDS.

THE AUTHOR OF "MARY HAD A LITTLE LAMB" IS RESPONSIBLE FOR MAKING THANKSGIVING A NATIONAL HOLIDAY.

THERE ARE 293 WAYS TO MAKE CHANGE FOR A DOLLAR.

UMBRELLAS WERE ONCE ONLY USED BY WOMEN.

ONLY FEMALE MOSQUITOES BITE.

Only female mosquitoes bite people and animals to get a blood meal. Female mosquitoes need a blood meal to produce eggs. Mosquitoes get infected with germs, such as viruses and parasites, when they bite infected people and animals.

123456 IS THE MOST COMMON PASSWORD.

Q IS THE ONLY LETTER THAT DOESN'T APPEAR IN ANY AMERICAN STATE NAME.

YOU MIGHT BE DRINKING WATER THAT IS OLDER THAN THE SOLAR SYSTEM.

ALASKA IS THE ONLY STATE WHOSE NAME IS ON ONE ROW ON A KEYBOARD.

A CAT'S JAW CANNOT MOVE SIDEWAYS.

Cats can fit into any opening of the size of their head because they don't have a collarbone. Cats can't chew large chunks of food because their jaws are unable to move sideways.

NO TWO TIGERS HAVE THE SAME STRIPE PATTERN.

IN WELSH FOLKLORE, CORGIS CARRIED FAIRIES.

Welsh legend says the fairies and elves of Wales used the Pembroke Welsh Corgi to pull fairy coaches, work fairy cattle, and serve as the steed for fairy warriors. If you look closely, even today you can see the marks of the "fairy saddle" over the shoulders in the Pembroke's coat.

KOTEX WAS FIRST MANUFACTURED AS BANDAGES, DURING WWI.

ALFRED HITCHCOCK DIDN'T HAVE A BELLYBUTTON.

THE WORLD'S LARGEST NATIONAL PARK IS LOCATED IN GREENLAND.

AIRPORT RUNWAY NUMBERS INDICATE THE DIRECTION ON A COMPASS.

SNAILS TAKE THE LONGEST NAPS WITH SOME LASTING AS LONG AS THREE YEARS.

Snails need moisture to survive, so if the weather is not cooperating, they can actually sleep up to three years. It has been reported that depending on geography, snails can shift into hibernation (which occurs in the winter), or estivation (also known as "summer sleep"), helping to escape warm climates.

THE CANARY ISLANDS ARE NAMED AFTER DOGS, NOT BIRDS.

THE PARIS AGREEMENT ON CLIMATE CHANGE WAS SIGNED BY THE LARGEST NUMBER OF COUNTRIES EVER IN ONE DAY.

PITTSBURGH IS THE ONLY CITY WHERE ALL THE MAJOR SPORTS TEAMS (MLB, NHL, NFL) HAVE THE SAME COLORS: BLACK AND GOLD.

AUTHOR ROALD DAHL WAS A SPY.

COTTON CANDY WAS INVENTED BY A DENTIST.

FRENCH POODLES ARE ACTUALLY FROM GERMANY.

BILL GATES HAS DONATED NEARLY HALF HIS FORTUNE.

SLINKIES ARE 82 FEET LONG.

BLOOD BANKS IN SWEDEN NOTIFY DONORS WHEN BLOOD IS USED.

THE "M'S" IN M&MS STAND FOR "MARS" AND "MURRIE."

THE WORLD WASTES ABOUT ONE BILLION METRIC TONS OF FOOD EACH YEAR.

HIGH HEELS WERE ORIGINALLY WORN BY MEN.

High-heeled shoes were first worn by Persian soldiers in the 10th century to elevate their feet, giving them stability while shooting their bows and arrows. Since then, men heels symbolize high social stature, military power and fashionable taste.

GOLF IS THE ONLY
SPORT TO BE PLAYED
ON THE MOON.

CREEDENCE CLEARWATER REVIVAL HAS THE MOST NO. 2 BILLBOARD HITS, WITHOUT EVER HITTING NO. 1.

GOATS HAVE RECTANGULAR PUPILS IN THEIR EYES.

PILOTS AND THEIR CO-PILOTS ARE REQUIRED TO EAT DIFFERENT MEALS BEFORE FLIGHTS SO THAT THEY DON'T BOTH END UP WITH FOOD POISONING.

LESS THAN 5% OF THE OCEANS HAVE BEEN EXPLORED BY HUMANS.

The oceans account for 70 percent of Earth's surface. In other words, humans haven't yet explored or discovered about 65 percent of Earth's surface area.

MONACO'S ORCHESTRA IS BIGGER THAN ITS ARMY.

THE DARK REGION ON THE NORTH POLE OF PLUTO'S MOON, CHARON, IS CALLED MORDOR.

BEFORE TOILET PAPER WAS INVENTED, AMERICANS USED TO USE CORN COBS.

SLOTHS CAN HOLD THEIR BREATH LONGER THAN DOLPHINS CAN.

Amazingly, sloths can hold their breath for over 20 minutes—some have even reported up to 40—by slowing their heart rate. Dolphins, on the other hand, can usually only manage around 10 minutes underwater.

DR. SEUSS INVENTED THE WORD "NERD."

JACK DANIEL DIED FROM A TOE INJURY.

THE LEANING TOWER OF PISA IS TILTED DUE TO THE SOIL AT ITS BASE.

THE WORLD'S LARGEST WATERFALL IS UNDERWATER AT THE DENMARK STRAIT.

HUMMINGBIRDS ARE THE ONLY ANIMALS THAT CAN FLY BACKWARDS.

THERE ARE 31,556,926 SECONDS IN A YEAR.

BIG BEN IN LONDON IS LEANING SO MUCH THAT THE INCLINE IS VISIBLE TO THE NAKED EYE.

Experts say the world-famous neogothic clock tower is listing gently, and documents recently published by Britain's Parliament show that the top of its gilded spire is about 18 inches out of line.

YOU'RE BORN WITH JUST 1 PINT OF BLOOD, BUT BY THE TIME YOU'RE AN ADULT YOU HAVE 4 TO 5 QUARTS.

THE TALLEST PLAYER IN THE NHL IS ZDENO CHARA, WHO IS 6 FT. 9 IN. TALL.

SALMON P. CHASE WAS THE FIRST FACE ON THE DOLLAR BILL.

Salmon P. Chase graced the front of the first dollar bill, which was issued in 1862. As the treasury secretary under President Abraham Lincoln, he was a fitting choice to usher in this new and modern type of paper currency.

NEPTUNE'S DAYS ARE 16 HOURS LONG.

CANDY CORN WAS ORIGINALLY CALLED CHICKEN FEED.

ELVIS WAS ORIGINALLY BLOND. HE STARTED COLORING HIS HAIR BLACK FOR AN EDGIER LOOK.

PRINGLES AREN'T ACTUALLY POTATO CHIPS.

BRUNCH WAS ORIGINALLY INVENTED TO CURE HANGOVERS.

YOU CAN LEARN THE HIGH VALYRIAN LANGUAGE FROM GAME OF THRONES WITH AN ONLINE COURSE.

YOUR SMALL INTESTINE IS THE LARGEST INTERNAL ORGAN IN YOUR BODY.

Although the small intestine is narrower than the large intestine, it is actually the longest section of your digestive tube, measuring about 22 feet (or seven meters) on average, or three and a half times the length of your body.

MALE STUDENTS AT BRIGHAM YOUNG UNIVERSITY IN UTAH NEED SPECIAL PERMISSION TO GROW A BEARD.

Students must formally petition for exemptions based on medical, theatrical or religious needs.

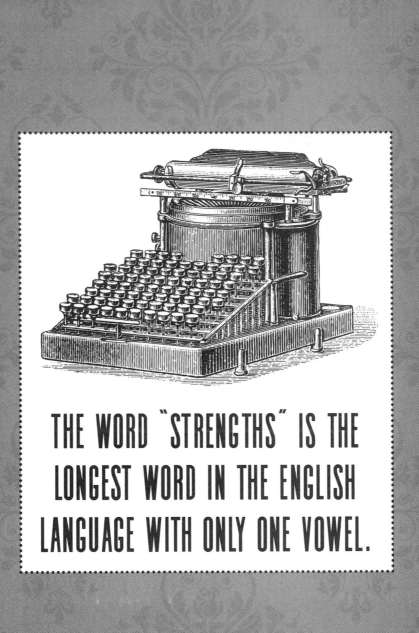

THE WORD "STRENGTHS" IS THE LONGEST WORD IN THE ENGLISH LANGUAGE WITH ONLY ONE VOWEL.

THE HEADS ON EASTER ISLAND HAVE BODIES.

Archaeologists have uncovered the bodies associated with the heads and found interesting discoveries that further our knowledge of the Easter Island civilization and how they created the monoliths.

THE BEATLES USED THE WORD "LOVE" 613 TIMES IN THEIR SONGS.

EUGENE LAZOWSKI, A POLISH DOCTOR, ONCE FAKED AN OUTBREAK TO KEEP THE NAZIS AWAY, SAVING 8,000 PEOPLE.

STOP SIGNS USED TO BE YELLOW.

ONE QUARTER OF ALL YOUR BONES ARE LOCATED IN YOUR FEET.

NINTENDO TRADEMARKED THE PHRASE "IT'S ON LIKE DONKEY KONG" IN 2010.

A CHEF'S HAT HAS EXACTLY 100 PLEATS.

BUCKINGHAM PALACE IN LONDON, ENGLAND, HAS 775 ROOMS, INCLUDING 78 BATHROOMS.

GATORADE WAS NAMED AFTER THE UNIVERSITY OF FLORIDA GATORS.

A group of doctors invented the drink in a science lab on University of Florida's campus in 1965 (hence the name, inspired by the Florida Gators).

EVERY TIME YOU SHUFFLE A DECK OF CARDS, YOU GET A COMBINATION THAT'S NEVER EXISTED.

DANIEL RADCLIFFE WAS ALLERGIC TO HIS HARRY POTTER GLASSES BECAUSE OF THE NICKEL.

During the filming of the first episode of the saga, Harry Potter and the Philosopher's Stone, he developed an allergy at the contact of the eyeglasses of his character: a rash shaped in two perfect circles around his eyes.

IN EVERY SCENE OF
FIGHT CLUB, THERE
IS A STARBUCKS
COFFEE CUP.

APRIL 11, 1954, WAS RECORDED AS THE MOST BORING DAY IN THE WORLD.

SELFIES KILL MORE PEOPLE THAN SHARKS.

THE FULLER THE FRIDGE, THE MORE ENERGY-EFFICIENT IT IS.

THE STRAWBERRY IS THE ONLY FRUIT THAT BEARS SEEDS ON THE OUTSIDE.

HAWAIIAN PIZZA IS CANADIAN.

IT'S IMPOSSIBLE TO BURP IN SPACE.

On Earth, gravity causes the liquids and gasses in your digestive system to separate. The liquids are more dense, so they sink. The gasses sit on top. So, when you belch, you expel only gasses. In microgravity, the liquids and gasses do not separate in that manner, so when you belch, there is a good chance you will expel some liquids.

AUSTRALIA HAS THE MOST BEACHES IN THE WORLD.

Australia's coastline stretches almost 50,000 kilometers and is linked by over 10,000 beaches, more than any other country in the world.

AFTER WORKING AT BASKIN-ROBBINS AS A TEEN, FORMER PRESIDENT OBAMA DISLIKES ICE CREAM.

JAMES CAMERON DREW THAT CHARCOAL OF KATE WINSLET.

A GIRAFFE CAN GO LONGER WITHOUT WATER THAN A CAMEL CAN.

ANIMALS THAT LAY EGGS DON'T HAVE BELLY BUTTONS.

GRAPES EXPLODE WHEN YOU PUT THEM IN THE MICROWAVE.

THERE ARE NO CLOCKS IN LAS VEGAS GAMBLING CASINOS.

Casinos don't have clocks or windows because they want to keep players focused on playing games. Casinos make more money the longer you play and clocks distract players by giving them a reference for how long they have been playing.

ABRAHAM LINCOLN IS IN THE WRESTLING HALL OF FAME.

Abraham Lincoln was a skilled wrestler and was honored with an award from the National Wrestling Hall of Fame in 1992.

THE HEART OF A SHRIMP IS LOCATED IN ITS HEAD.

AN OSTRICH'S EYE IS BIGGER THAN ITS BRAIN.

The ostrich is the largest bird in the world and has the largest eyes in the whole animal kingdom. An ostrich's eyes are bigger than its brain—about 2 inches (5 centimeters) in diameter, almost the size of a billiard ball.

AROUND 50% OF THE MINED GOLD ON EARTH COMES FROM A PLATEAU IN SOUTH AFRICA.

DR PEPPER DOES NOT HAVE A PERIOD.

SAINT LUCIA IS THE ONLY COUNTRY IN THE WORLD NAMED AFTER A WOMAN.

THE SNOW ON VENUS IS METAL.

At the very top of Venus's mountains, beneath the thick clouds, is a layer of snow. But since it's so hot on Venus, snow as we know it can't exist. Instead, the snow-capped mountains are capped with two types of metal: galena and bismuthinite.

ONLY ABOUT 100 PEOPLE SPEAK LATIN FLUENTLY.

THREE CONSECUTIVE STRIKES IN BOWLING IS CALLED A TURKEY.

THE MOST COMMON NAME IN THE WORLD IS MOHAMMED.

THE PLASTIC TIPS OF SHOELACES ARE CALLED AGLETS.

ELEPHANTS SUCK ON THEIR TRUNKS FOR COMFORT.

ANDREW JACKSON HAD A VULGAR PARROT NAMED POLLY.

America's seventh president was never known for his personal restraint, and it seems that Andrew Jackson's propensity for swear words rubbed off on his pet parrot. Contemporary accounts suggest that the parrot, agitated by the crowds attending Jackson's funeral at his home in 1845, launched into a profane tirade while surrounded by mourners.

BLUE IVY CARTER IS THE YOUNGEST PERSON EVER TO APPEAR ON A BILLBOARD CHART.

The daughter of Beyoncé and JAY-Z made her debut on the Billboard Hot 100, reaching number 76 with "Brown Skin Girl" from her mother's just-released soundtrack album The Lion King: The Gift.

ANTARCTICA IS THE ONLY CONTINENT WITHOUT ANY REPTILES OR SNAKES.

THE LARGEST SNOWFLAKE ON RECORD WAS 15 INCHES WIDE.

TED DANSON ACTUALLY WENT TO TWO WEEKS OF BARTENDING SCHOOL TO PREPARE FOR HIS ROLE ON CHEERS.

YOU CAN EAT THE STICKERS ON FRUIT.

ONLY ONE CAPITAL IN THE U.S. HAS NO MCDONALD'S: MONTPELIER, VT.

VALENTINE'S DAY STARTED AS A ROMAN REBELLION.

CANADIANS SAY "SORRY" SO MUCH THAT A LAW WAS PASSED IN 2009 DECLARING THAT AN APOLOGY CAN'T BE USED AS EVIDENCE OF ADMISSION TO GUILT.

THE LORD OF THE RINGS: THE RETURN OF THE KING WON ALL 11 ACADEMY AWARDS IT WAS NOMINATED FOR.

NO WORD IN THE ENGLISH LANGUAGE RHYMES WITH "MONTH."

FISHING IS THE BIGGEST PARTICIPANT SPORT IN THE WORLD.

THE QUEEN OWNS ALL THE SWANS IN ENGLAND.

According to the official Royal Family website, the Crown has held the right to claim ownership of all unmarked mute swans swimming in open waters across the country since the 12th Century.

INTERNATIONAL ASTRONAUTS MUST BE ABLE TO SPEAK RUSSIAN.

MISS PIGGY WAS ORIGINALLY NAMED PIGGY LEE.

SHARKS EXISTED BEFORE TREES.

POPE JOHN PAUL II WAS AN HONORARY HARLEM GLOBETROTTER.

THE LOGO FOR CHUPA CHUPS WAS DESIGNED BY SALVADOR DALÍ.

THE TERM "BRAH" IS HAWAIIAN PIDGIN, SHORT FOR BRAHDAH (BROTHER).

THE FIRST PERSON SELECTED AS THE TIME MAGAZINE MAN OF THE YEAR WAS CHARLES LINDBERGH IN 1927.

SHEL SILVERSTEIN WROTE THE SONG "A BOY NAMED SUE."

"A Boy Named Sue" is a song written by humorist, children's author, and poet Shel Silverstein and made popular by Johnny Cash. Cash recorded the song live in concert on February 24, 1969 at California's San Quentin State Prison for his At San Quentin album.

VENUS IS THE ONLY PLANET TO SPIN CLOCKWISE.

THE IKEA CATALOG IS THE MOST WIDELY PRINTED BOOK IN HISTORY.

BUZZ'S GIRLFRIEND WAS ACTUALLY A BOY MADE UP LIKE A GIRL IN HOME ALONE.

BATS EAT 3,000 INSECTS A NIGHT.

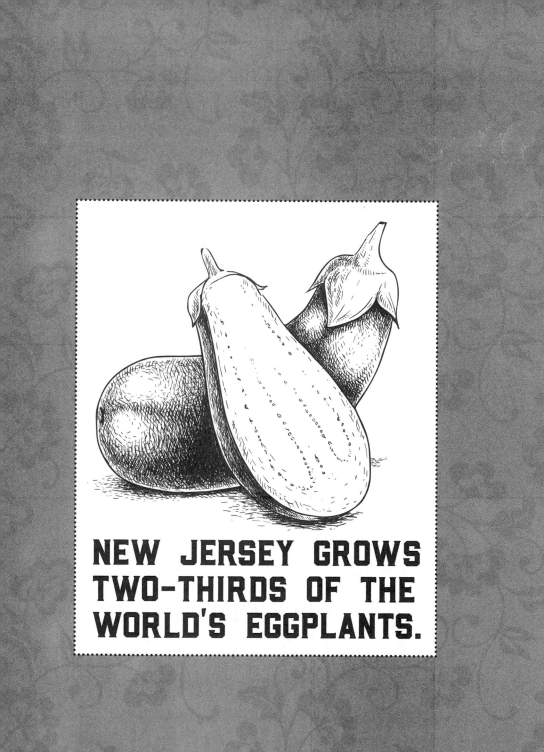

NEW JERSEY GROWS
TWO-THIRDS OF THE
WORLD'S EGGPLANTS.

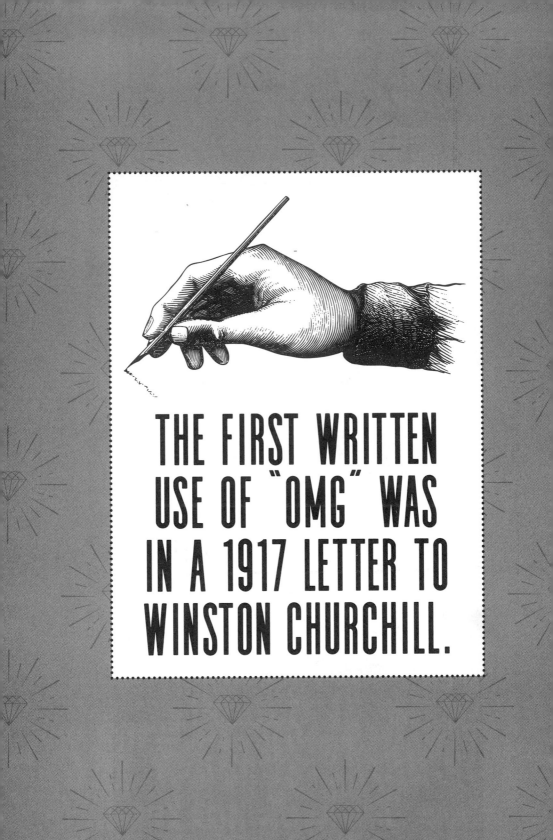

THE FIRST WRITTEN USE OF ˝OMG˝ WAS IN A 1917 LETTER TO WINSTON CHURCHILL.

YOU CAN'T BRING A FURBY TO THE PENTAGON.

In 1999, Furbys were officially banned by the NSA, the Norfolk Naval Shipyard, and the Pentagon. Administrators allegedly worried that an employee might bring one into work wherein it could eavesdrop on a top-secret conversation and "start talking classified."

DURING WORLD WAR II, THE OSCAR AWARDS WERE MADE OF PAINTED PLASTER.

THE SILHOUETTE ON THE NBA LOGO IS OF HALL OF FAME LOS ANGELES LAKER JERRY WEST.

TWO BILLION PEOPLE ON EARTH EAT INSECTS AS PART OF THEIR REGULAR DIET.

"AVIATION ENGLISH" IS THE LANGUAGE ALL PILOTS SPEAK NO MATTER WHAT THEIR NATIONALITY IS.

TOMATOES HAVE MORE GENES THAN HUMANS.

Plant geneticists from 14 different countries have discovered that the tomato contains 31,760 genes—that's 7,000 more genes than a human being!

THE ORIGINAL STANLEY CUP WAS ONLY 7.5 INCHES HIGH.

THE REAL ST. PATRICK WAS BORN IN BRITAIN.

45% OF AMERICANS MAKE NEW YEAR'S RESOLUTIONS.

PRESIDENT JOHN TYLER HAD 15 CHILDREN.

President John Tyler had 15 children. Eight were with his first wife, Lettia Tyler, and the other seven were with his second wife, Julia Gardiner.

WALT DISNEY CURRENTLY HOLDS THE MOST ACADEMY AWARDS.

YOU NEED 10 YEARS OF CHEESE MAKING EXPERIENCE TO BECOME A MASTER CHEESEMAKER IN WISCONSIN.

Wisconsin is the sole state where you can be crowned a certified Master Cheesemaker. But before any of that happens (a process involving a three-year course of study and a practical apprenticeship), an inductee will need to have possessed a cheesemaker's license in Wisconsin for at least 10 years.

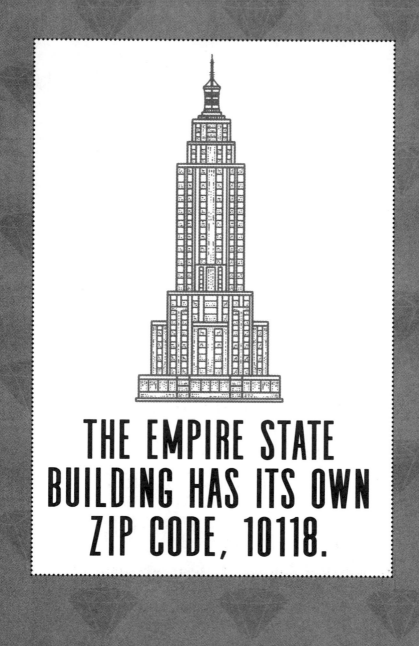

THE EMPIRE STATE BUILDING HAS ITS OWN ZIP CODE, 10118.

EATING POLAR BEAR LIVER
CAN KILL A HUMAN BEING
BECAUSE OF ITS HIGH
CONCENTRATION OF VITAMIN A.

BUFFY THE VAMPIRE SLAYER WAS THE FIRST SHOW TO USE THE WORD "GOOGLE" AS A VERB ON TV.

HOT WATER FREEZES FASTER THAN COLD WATER.

If the water is initially hot, cooled water at the bottom is denser than the hot water at the top, so no convection will occur and the bottom part will start freezing while the top is still warm.

THE ORIGINAL STAR WARS PREMIERED ON JUST 32 SCREENS ACROSS THE U.S. IN 1977.

RENO IS FARTHER WEST THAN LOS ANGELES.

PORTUGAL IS THE TOP COUNTRY FOR CORK PRODUCTION.

Portugal is the center of the world's cork business. That country has roughly 1.6 million acres of cork forests, representing 30% of the world's cork trees.

THE SPICE GIRLS
WERE ORIGINALLY A
BAND CALLED TOUCH.

THE LARGEST LIVING ORGANISM IS AN ASPEN GROVE IN UTAH CALLED PANDO.

Pando is believed to be the largest, most dense organism ever found at nearly 13 million pounds. The clone spreads over 106 acres, consisting of over 40,000 individual trees.

40% OF MCDONALD'S PROFITS COME FROM THE SALES OF HAPPY MEALS.

FEBRUARY USED TO BE THE LAST MONTH OF THE YEAR.

CARDS AGAINST HUMANITY BOUGHT AN ISLAND IN MAINE TO PRESERVE WILDLIFE. IT IS CALLED HAWAII 2.

Hawaii 2 (previously Birch Island) is a six-acre private island in Maine's St. George Lake. Previously used as de facto public land, in 2014 the island was purchased by Cards Against Humanity LLC as part of a fundraiser for the Sunlight Foundation.

ONLY 3 COUNTRIES DON'T USE THE METRIC SYSTEM: MYANMAR, LIBERIA AND THE UNITED STATES.

JOHN ADAMS WAS THE FIRST PRESIDENT TO LIVE IN THE WHITE HOUSE.

Construction began when the first cornerstone was laid in October of 1792. Although President Washington oversaw the construction of the house, he never lived in it. It was not until 1800, when the White House was nearly completed, that its first residents, President John Adams and his wife, Abigail, moved in.

AVOCADOS DON'T RIPEN IN TREES. THEY HAVE TO BE PLUCKED FIRST.

Avocados are mature before picking, but not ready to eat. They must be softened off the tree. The softening process takes from a few days to a week, depending upon the degree of maturity, storage temperature and variety.

GORILLAS CAN CATCH HUMAN COLDS.

THE SPIKED DOG COLLARS ARE MEANT TO PROTECT THEIR NECKS FROM ATTACKS.

THE HOTTEST TEMPERATURE EVER RECORDED OCCURRED IN FURNACE CREEK, DEATH VALLEY, CALIFORNIA, AT 134 DEGREES FAHRENHEIT.

FLIPPING A SHARK UPSIDE DOWN RENDERS IT IMMOBILE FOR UP TO 15 MINUTES.

Once sharks are upside down, it doesn't take long for tonic immobility to kick in. It usually takes no more than 60 seconds to render a shark motionless. If nothing interferes with their tonic immobility, it can last for a maximum of 15 minutes or so.

METALLICA IS THE FIRST BAND TO HAVE PLAYED ON ALL 7 CONTINENTS.

THE "WAFFLE HOUSE INDEX" IS INFORMALLY USED BY FEMA TO MEASURE STORM SEVERITY.

COPPER DOOR KNOBS ARE SELF–DISINFECTING.

TABLE TENNIS BALLS CAN TRAVEL OFF THE PADDLE AT 105.6 MILES PER HOUR.

A BOLT OF LIGHTNING CONTAINS ENOUGH ENERGY TO TOAST 100,000 SLICES OF BREAD.

AMERICA ACCIDENTALLY DROPPED AN ATOM BOMB ON SOUTH CAROLINA IN 1958.

The bomb was a 26-kiloton Mark 6, a more powerful version of the Fat Man dropped on Nagasaki. It mistakenly fell out of a B-47 jet, dropping 15,000 feet into the back yard of Walter Gregg and his family. The plutonium core didn't explode, but the 6,000 pounds of conventional high explosives detonated, transforming the Greggs' vegetable garden into a vast muddy crater and destroying their house.

VISITORS ARE NOT ALLOWED TO SCATTER LOVED ONES' ASHES AT DISNEY WORLD OR DISNEYLAND.

THE WORD "FRIENDS" IS SAID IN EVERY EPISODE OF FRIENDS.

THE POKEMON RHYDON WAS THE FIRST ONE TO BE CREATED.

WILLIAM MCKINLEY WAS SHOT RIGHT AFTER GIVING AWAY HIS GOOD-LUCK CHARM, A RED CARNATION.

MIAMI IS THE ONLY MAJOR U.S. CITY FOUNDED BY A WOMAN.

OCTOPUSES HAVE THREE HEARTS.

Octopuses have three hearts, which is partly a consequence of having blue blood. Their two peripheral hearts pump blood through the gills, where it picks up oxygen. A central heart then circulates the oxygenated blood to the rest of the body to provide energy for organs and muscles.

THE TWITTER BIRD'S OFFICIAL NAME IS LARRY.

ALICE COOPER IS AN AVID GOLFER.

THE ONLY DIFFERENCE BETWEEN KOSHER SALT AND TABLE SALT IS THE GRAIN SIZE.

The most striking difference between Kosher salt and regular salt is just the grain size. If you look at table salt under a microscope, you'll see that table salt has been milled such that many of the salt crystals look like little cubes.

MLB UMPIRES ARE REQUIRED TO WEAR BLACK UNDERWEAR IN CASE THEY SPLIT THEIR PANTS.

THE LAST LETTER ADDED TO THE ALPHABET WAS ACTUALLY "J."

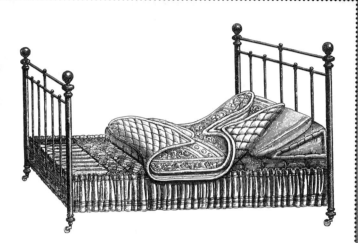

CHARLES DICKENS ALWAYS HAD HIS BED FACING NORTH.

Charles Dickens always slept facing north, in an effort to battle insomnia – when he travelled, he would carry a compass with him and move his bed around so it was correctly aligned. He also liked to face north while writing, believing it aided his creativity.

GEORGE WASHINGTON OPENED A WHISKEY DISTILLERY AFTER HIS PRESIDENCY.

In 1799, George Washington's distillery produced nearly 11,000 gallons, making it one of the largest whiskey distilleries in America.

JULIE ANDREWS LEARNED TO PLAY THE GUITAR FOR THE SOUND OF MUSIC.

THE CLEVELAND BROWNS ARE THE ONLY TEAM TO NEITHER PLAY IN NOR HOST A SUPERBOWL.

THE SUPER SOAKER WAS DESIGNED AND INVENTED BY A NASA ENGINEER.

SONIC THE HEDGEHOG'S FULL NAME IS OGILVIE MAURICE HEDGEHOG.

AT AGE 23, EVAN SPIEGEL, THE FOUNDER OF SNAPCHAT, IS THE WORLD'S YOUNGEST BILLIONAIRE.

COLD WATER IS JUST AS CLEANSING AS HOT WATER.

SHAQ ONLY MADE ONE THREE-POINTER IN HIS CAREER.

A SINGLE STRAND OF SPAGHETTI IS INDIVIDUALLY REFERRED TO AS SPAGHETTO.

JERRY SPRINGER WAS BORN IN A LONDON SUBWAY STATION DURING WORLD WAR II.

THE DIRECTORS OF THE FILM DESPICABLE ME WROTE THEIR OWN LANGUAGE FOR THE MINIONS.

Minionese, as it's known, is a constructed language created by Despicable Me co-directors Pierre Coffin and Chris Renaud. While it may sound like incoherent babbling, the practically indistinguishable words are actually a handcrafted dialect specifically designed for the Minions.

THE FASTEST MAN IN THE WORLD, USAIN BOLT, HAS SCOLIOSIS.

NASCAR DRIVERS CAN LOSE UP TO 10 POUNDS IN SWEAT DUE TO HIGH TEMPERATURES DURING RACES.

THE MAJORITY OF YOUR BRAIN IS FAT.

The human brain is nearly 60 percent fat. We've learned in recent years that fatty acids are among the most crucial molecules that determine your brain's integrity and ability to perform.

INSTEAD OF SAYING "CHEESE"
BEFORE TAKING A PICTURE,
VICTORIANS SAID "PRUNES."

THE MAN WHO FOUNDED ATARI ALSO STARTED CHUCK E. CHEESE.

Before he turned 40, Nolan Bushnell founded two brands that permanently shaped the way Americans amuse themselves: the iconic video game system Atari, and the frenetic family restaurant Chuck E. Cheese's.

"E" IS THE MOST COMMON LETTER AND APPEARS IN 11 PERCENT OF ALL ENGLISH WORDS.

THE AVERAGE PERSON WILL SPEND SIX MONTHS OF THEIR LIFE WAITING FOR RED LIGHTS TO TURN GREEN.

GIANT PANDAS EAT APPROXIMATELY 28 POUNDS OF BAMBOO A DAY.

AT LEAST ONE OF THE COLORS OF THE OLYMPIC FLAG APPEARS ON ALL THE NATIONAL FLAGS.

ONE IN THREE DIVORCE FILINGS INCLUDE THE WORD "FACEBOOK."

A third of all divorce filings in 2011 contained the word "Facebook," according to Divorce Online. And more than 80 percent of U.S. divorce attorneys say social networking in divorce proceedings is on the rise, according to the American Academy of Matrimonial Lawyers.

SWEDEN HAS 267,570 ISLANDS, THE MOST OF ANY COUNTRY IN THE WORLD.

CANS OF DIET SODA WILL FLOAT IN WATER BUT REGULAR SODA CANS WILL SINK.

CHEESE IS THE MOST SHOPLIFTED FOOD IN THE WORLD.

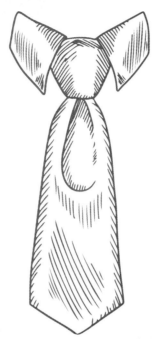

THE MOST COMMON GIFT ON FATHER'S DAY IS A NECKTIE.

PAUL REVERE NEVER ACTUALLY SHOUTED, "THE BRITISH ARE COMING!"

Paul Revere never shouted the legendary phrase later attributed to him as he passed from town to town. The operation was meant to be conducted as discreetly as possible since scores of British troops were hiding out in the Massachusetts countryside.

BULLFROGS DO NOT SLEEP.

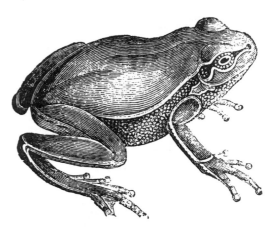

RED SOUR PATCH KIDS ARE THE EXACT SAME CANDY AS SWEDISH FISH, JUST WITH SOME SOUR SUGAR SPRINKLED ON THEM.

WILLIAM SHAKESPEARE HAD A CURSE ENGRAVED ON HIS TOMBSTONE TO PREVENT ANYONE FROM MOVING HIS BONES.

MAJOR LEAGUE BASEBALL TEAMS USE ABOUT 850,000 BALLS PER SEASON.

ICELAND HAS A DATING APP THAT STOPS YOU FROM HOOKING UP WITH YOUR COUSIN.

PIGS DON'T SWEAT.

Pigs do not sweat but they are able to rid themselves of heat in other ways such as via their skin and through respiration.

BABE RUTH WORE A CABBAGE LEAF UNDER HIS CAP TO KEEP HIS HEAD COOL. HE CHANGED IT EVERY TWO INNINGS.

NFL SUPER BOWL REFEREES ALSO GET SUPER BOWL RINGS.

POPE FRANCIS USED TO BE A NIGHTCLUB BOUNCER.

Pope Francis, then known as Jorge Mario Bergoglio, worked as a bouncer, a janitor sweeping floors and a chemical tester in a laboratory before becoming a priest.

THERE ARE MORE LEGO MINI-FIGURES THAN THERE ARE PEOPLE ON EARTH.

FOUR OUT OF THE TEN LARGEST STATUES IN THE WORLD ARE OF BUDDHAS.

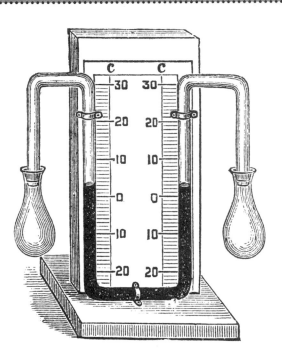

BEFORE MERCURY, BRANDY WAS USED TO FILL THERMOMETERS.

Some of the earliest thermometers contained brandy instead of mercury. The liquor was eventually replaced with mercury due to the latter material's wider range of liquid-state temperature.

THE LINE BETWEEN THE NUMBERS IN A FRACTION IS THE VINCULUM.

APPLESAUCE WAS THE FIRST FOOD EATEN IN SPACE BY ASTRONAUTS.

THE WORLD'S MOST EXPENSIVE DESSERT FROM NEW YORK CITY'S SERENDIPITY 3 CAFE CAME IN AT A WHOPPING $25,000.

CHINA DIDN'T WIN ITS FIRST OLYMPIC MEDAL UNTIL 1984.

HERSHEY'S CHOCOLATE SYRUP, RITZ CRACKERS, DUMDUMS, AND OREOS ARE ALL VEGAN.

TOTO WAS PAID $125 PER WEEK WHILE FILMING THE WIZARD OF OZ.

In the 1939 movie The Wizard of Oz, Toto was played by a female brindle Cairn Terrier named Terry. She was paid a $125 salary each week, which was more than some of the human actors.

SANTA CLAUS ORIGINATED IN A NEWSPAPER AD.

3 OUT OF 4 AMERICANS USE AN EMOJI IN TEXT MESSAGING EVERY SINGLE DAY.

YOU CAN SEE FOUR STATES FROM THE TOP OF CHICAGO'S WILLIS TOWER.

THE FIRST CD PRESSED IN THE U.S. WAS BRUCE SPRINGSTEEN'S "BORN IN THE USA."

THERE WAS A SUCCESSFUL TINDER MATCH IN ANTARCTICA IN 2014.

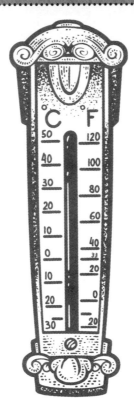

THE COLDEST TEMPERATURE EVER
RECORDED OCCURRED IN ANTARCTICA,
−144 FAHRENHEIT.

PEACHES ARE MEMBERS OF THE ALMOND FAMILY.

THE BARBIE DOLL'S FULL NAME IS BARBARA MILLICENT ROBERTS, FROM WILLOWS, WISCONSIN.

JIM CARREY AUDITIONED TO BE A CAST MEMBER OF SNL MULTIPLE TIMES, BUT WAS NEVER HIRED.

ABERCROMBIE & FITCH PAID MTV TO MAKE SURE THE CAST OF JERSEY SHORE DOESN'T WEAR THEIR CLOTHES.

3 DOGS SURVIVED THE SINKING OF THE TITANIC.

The three dogs that survived had a few things in common: they were being kept in staterooms, not in the kennel, and they were tiny. They were taken into lifeboats by their owners, most likely wrapped in blankets or tucked under a coat.

CANADA EATS MORE MACARONI AND CHEESE THAN ANY OTHER NATION IN THE WORLD.

JOUSTING IS THE OFFICIAL SPORT IN THE STATE OF MARYLAND.

ALLODOXAPHOBIA IS THE FEAR OF OPINIONS.

The word allodoxaphobia can be considered a derivative of doxophobia though the two words have contradictory meanings. Where doxophobia stands for the fear of expressing opinions, allodoxaphobia is the fear of hearing other people's opinions.

GUINNESS WORLD RECORDS WAS FOUNDED BY THE MANAGING DIRECTOR OF GUINNESS BREWERY IN THE 1950S.

WOMEN COULDN'T APPLY FOR CREDIT AT A BANK UNTIL 1974.

Banks could refuse women a credit card until the Equal Credit Opportunity Act of 1974 was signed into law. Prior to that, a bank could refuse to issue a credit card to an unmarried woman, and if a woman was married, her husband was required to cosign.

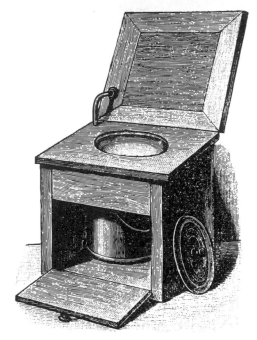

IN SWITZERLAND, IT IS ILLEGAL TO FLUSH THE TOILET AFTER 10PM.

It's not only illegal to flush the toilet after 10pm if you're in an apartment, but also illegal for men to urinate standing up late at night.

CAMEL'S MILK DOESN'T CURDLE.

Due to its composition, camel milk does not curdle naturally and won't coagulate as easily as other types of milk.

J IS THE ONLY LETTER IN THE ENGLISH ALPHABET THAT CANNOT BE FOUND ON THE PERIODIC TABLE.

THREE PRESIDENTS, ALL FOUNDING FATHERS—JOHN ADAMS, THOMAS JEFFERSON, AND JAMES MONROE—DIED ON JULY 4.

THE MOST LEAVES EVER FOUND ON A CLOVER IS 56.

MORE PEOPLE VISIT FRANCE THAN ANY OTHER COUNTRY.

BULLS CAN'T SEE RED.

Bulls, along with all other cattle, are color-blind to red. Thus, the bull is likely irritated not by the muleta's color, but by the cape's movement as the matador whips it around.

THE FIRST MOVIE EVER TO PUT OUT A MOTION-PICTURE SOUNDTRACK WAS SNOW WHITE AND THE SEVEN DWARFS.

THERE ARE 5 COUNTRIES IN THE WORLD THAT DON'T HAVE AIRPORTS: VATICAN CITY, SAN MARINO, MONACO, LIECHTENSTEIN, AND ANDORRA.

WITHOUT SALIVA, HUMANS ARE UNABLE TO TASTE FOOD.

KENTUCKY HAS MORE BARRELS OF BOURBON THAN PEOPLE.

Kentucky is the source of 95% of the world's bourbon. There are 4.7 million barrels of bourbon in Kentucky and only 4.3 million people.

MILLIE THE WHITE HOUSE DOG EARNED MORE THAN FOUR TIMES AS MUCH AS PRESIDENT BUSH IN 1991.

Millie's Book: As Dictated to Barbara Bush *is a 1990 children's book by Barbara Bush, written as if from the perspective of Millie the English Springer Spaniel. Post-tax proceeds from book sales were donated to a literacy nonprofit organization.*

IN 1907, A WOMAN WAS ARRESTED ON A BEACH IN BOSTON FOR WEARING A ONE-PIECE SWIMSUIT.

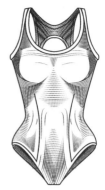

Australian swimmer Annette Kellerman was arrested in 1907 for stepping onto Revere Beach in the U.S. clad in a one-piece swimsuit that showed off her legs,

THE GOLDEN GIRLS' RUE MCCLANAHAN ALLEGEDLY KEPT ALL OF BLANCHE'S CLOTHES.

A FUNGUS IS MORE CLOSELY RELATED TO ANIMALS ON A GENETIC LEVEL THAN IT IS TO PLANTS.

Fungi and animals are more closely related to one another than either group is to plants. This has been determined through molecular phylogenetic analyses.

NEARLY ALL SPECIES TO HAVE EVER EXISTED ON EARTH ARE EXTINCT.

THE KILLERS' "MR. BRIGHTSIDE" LYRICS REPEAT BECAUSE OF PROCRASTINATION.

ALL PORCUPINES FLOAT IN WATER.

Porcupines are buoyant, in part due to the hollow structure of their quills. This helps porcupines float, but although North American, crested and brush-tailed porcupines are keen swimmers, not all porcupine species are fond of water.

WHEN KOKO THE GORILLA MET MR. ROGERS, SHE TOOK OFF HIS SHOES AS SHE HAD SEEN HIM DO ON HIS TV SHOW.

EYE OF NEWT, TOE OF FROG, AND WOOL OF BAT ARE JUST ARCHAIC TERMS FOR MUSTARD SEED, BUTTERCUP, AND HOLLY LEAVES.

4% OF THE SAND ON NORMANDY BEACH IS MADE UP OF SHRAPNEL FROM D—DAY THAT HAS BROKEN DOWN.

SEALS SLEEP ONLY ONE AND A HALF MINUTES AT A TIME.

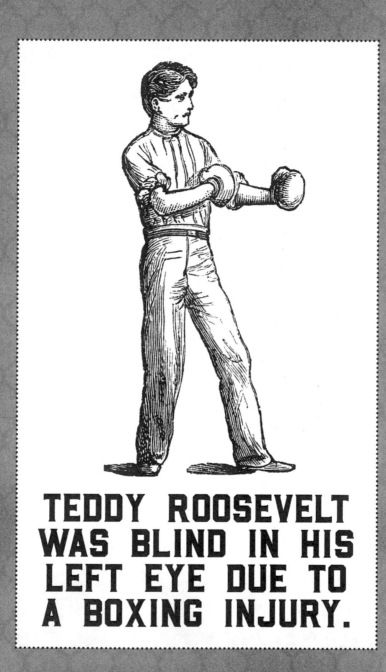

TEDDY ROOSEVELT
WAS BLIND IN HIS
LEFT EYE DUE TO
A BOXING INJURY.

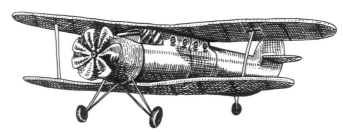

THE SHORTEST COMMERCIAL FLIGHT IN THE WORLD IS IN SCOTLAND WHICH IS 1.7 MILES.

The world's shortest commercial flight takes place between the two Orkney Islands, Westray and Papa Westray, just north of Scotland, separated by a distance of only 1.7 miles. Operated by Loganair, the flight duration is officially two minutes, but under ideal wind conditions can be completed in only 47 seconds.

THE COLLECTIVE NAME FOR A GROUP OF UNICORNS IS A BLESSING.

Seeing a unicorn is believed to bring good luck and fortune, which is why a group of unicorns is called a blessing.

HUMANS CANNOT WALK IN A STRAIGHT LINE WITHOUT A VISUAL POINT. WHEN BLINDFOLDED, WE WILL GRADUALLY WALK IN A CIRCLE.

IN AMERICA, IT IS A FEDERAL CRIME TO USE YOUR ROOMMATE OR FRIEND'S NETFLIX ACCOUNT.

IN ZIMBABWE, IT IS ILLEGAL FOR CITIZENS TO MAKE OFFENSIVE GESTURES AT A PASSING CAR.

LETTUCE IS A MEMBER OF THE SUNFLOWER FAMILY.

IN GREECE, WOMEN ARE NOT LEGALLY ALLOWED TO WEAR HIGH HEELS OR TALL HATS IN THE OLYMPIC STADIUM.

THE LONGEST ONE—SYLLABLE WORD IS "SCREECHED."

EVEN THOUGH SMOKING HAS BEEN BANNED ON AIRPLANES, ASHTRAYS ARE MANDATORY ON EVERY PLANE. THIS IS FOR SAFE DISPOSAL IN CASE SOMEONE BREAKS THE LAW.

IT SNOWED IN THE SAHARA DESERT FOR 30 MINUTES ON FEBRUARY 18, 1979.

DOGS CAN BE ALLERGIC TO HUMANS.

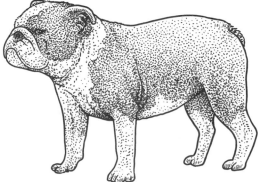

THERE ARE MORE STARS IN SPACE THAN THERE ARE GRAINS OF SAND ON EVERY BEACH IN THE WORLD.

Scientists estimate that Earth contains 7.5 sextillion sand grains. That is 75 followed by 17 zeros. Our universe contains at least 70 septillion stars, 7 followed by 23 zeros. Astronomers estimate there exist roughly 10,000 stars for each grain of sand on Earth.

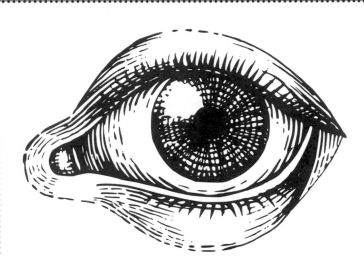

THE EYE MAKES MOVEMENTS 70–100 TIMES EVERY SECOND.

There is a typical eye movement called "cicadic movement." It is a tiny vibrating movement. It happens so fast that it appears you are looking at a whole object, but your eyes are moving 70 to 100 times per second all over.

ANOTHER TERM FOR YOUR NIECES OR NEPHEWS WOULD BE "NIBLINGS."

PIGEONS HAVE BEEN TRAINED BY THE U.S. COAST GUARD TO SPOT PEOPLE LOST AT SEA.

CUCUMBER CAN ACTUALLY CURE BAD BREATH.

A slice pressed to the roof of your mouth for 30 seconds with your tongue allows the phytochemicals to kill the problematic bacteria.

THE CAST OF FRIENDS STILL EARNS AROUND $20 MILLION EACH YEAR.

ASTRONAUTS ACTUALLY GET TALLER WHEN IN SPACE.

Astronauts in space can grow up to 3 percent taller during the time spent living in microgravity, NASA scientists say.

CANADIAN LAW REQUIRES CITIZENS TO ANSWER A MATH QUESTION WHEN ENTERING SWEEPSTAKES.

The Canadian courts have agreed that a four-part mathematical test such as "155 plus 33 minus four divided by 2" is enough to qualify as a skill-testing question, as long as winners are not allowed to use a calculator or other aid to answer the question.

IN UTAH, BIRDS HAVE THE RIGHT OF WAY ON A HIGHWAY.

AMY POEHLER WAS ONLY SEVEN YEARS OLDER THAN RACHEL MCADAMS WHEN SHE TOOK ON THE ROLE OF "COOL MOM" IN MEAN GIRLS.

PRINCE IS CREDITED WITH PLAYING 27 DIFFERENT INSTRUMENTS ON HIS DEBUT ALBUM.

PEOPLE IN NORTH KOREA ARE LEGALLY ONLY ALLOWED TO HAVE ONE OF 30 HAIRCUTS.

The North Korean government has approved 30 official hairstyles and all men and women in the country have to follow. Spiked hair is exclusively banned because the government thinks it's rebellious.

ERNEST HEMINGWAY'S
HOME IN KEY WEST HAS 54
CATS, MOSTLY POLYDACTYL.

IN ISRAEL, IT IS
ILLEGAL TO BRING
BEARS TO THE BEACH.

THE PUNCTUATION MARK ``?!'' IS CALLED AN INTERROBANG.

THE LARGEST LIVING THING ON EARTH IS A GIANT SEQUOIA NAMED GENERAL SHERMAN.

YOUR TONSILS CAN GROW BACK IF THERE WAS TISSUE LEFT BEHIND DURING THE REMOVAL PROCESS.

If you've had surgery to remove your tonsils—a procedure known as a tonsillectomy—it's possible for your tonsils to grow back. This can happen if tissue that gets left behind after the procedure regenerates. Typically, tonsils will regrow partially, but probably not completely.

JELLYFISH ARE CONSIDERED BIOLOGICALLY IMMORTAL. THEY DON'T AGE AND WILL NEVER DIE UNLESS THEY ARE KILLED.

VACUUM CLEANERS WERE ORIGINALLY HORSE—DRAWN.

THE NAME "BONOBO" RESULTED FROM A MISSPELLING.

"Bonobo," the common name for apes, may sound like some sort of translation of a meaningful term, but in fact, it was the result of a typo on the shipping crate in which the animal was placed.

ALFRED HITCHCOCK WAS FRIGHTENED OF EGGS.

SPIDER WEBS WERE USED AS BANDAGES IN ANCIENT TIMES.

THE LARGEST PADLOCK IN THE WORLD WEIGHS 916 POUNDS.

SQUIRRELS ARE BEHIND MOST POWER OUTAGES IN THE U.S.

SNAKES CAN HELP PREDICT EARTHQUAKES.

Snakes are some of the most sensitive beasts in the world. They can sense an upcoming major earthquake from 75 miles away. They can even sense the tremor 5 days before the earthquake occurs. When an earthquake is about to happen, they start behaving erratically and move out from their nests. If the tremor is major, they will try to escape.

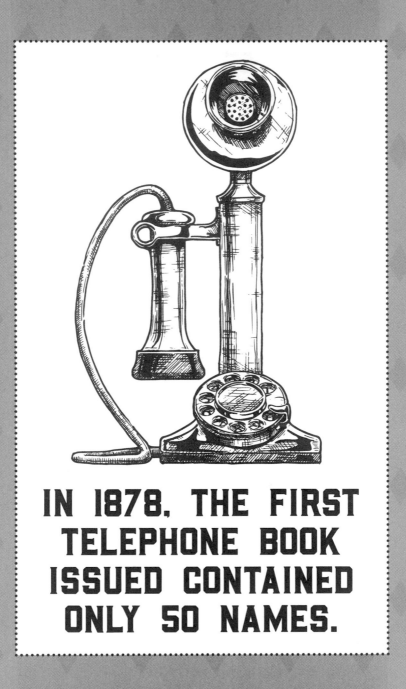

IN 1878, THE FIRST TELEPHONE BOOK ISSUED CONTAINED ONLY 50 NAMES.

IN THEIR LIFETIME, THE AVERAGE PERSON WALKS THE EQUIVALENT OF FIVE TIMES AROUND THE EARTH.

The average person with the average stride living until 80 will walk a distance of around 110,000 miles—which is the equivalent of walking about 5 times around the Earth, right on the equator.

HUMANS HAVE BEEN PERFORMING DENTISTRY SINCE 7000BC, WHICH MAKES DENTISTRY ONE OF THE OLDEST PROFESSIONS.

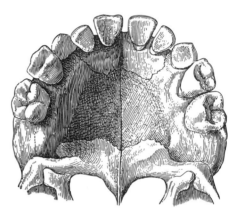

THE ORIGINAL FERRIS WHEEL WAS DESIGNED AND CONSTRUCTED IN CHICAGO, ILLINOIS, BY GEORGE WASHINGTON GALE FERRIS, JR.

DOLPHINS GIVE NAMES TO EACH OTHER.

Scientists have found further evidence that dolphins call each other by "name." Research has revealed that the marine mammals use a unique whistle to identify each other.

GOATS HAVE ACCENTS.

ANTEATERS HAVE NO TEETH.

TO KEEP FROM DRIFTING APART, SEA OTTERS HOLD HANDS WHILE THEY SLEEP.

HUMANS COULD NEVER ¨LAND¨ ON JUPITER, SATURN, URANUS OR NEPTUNE BECAUSE THEY ARE MADE OF GAS AND HAVE NO SOLID SURFACE.

THE FAMOUS LINE IN TITANIC FROM LEONARDO DICAPRIO, ¨I'M KING OF THE WORLD!¨ WAS IMPROVISED.

One of the movie's most iconic lines was improvised on the spot. Leonardo DiCaprio actually ad-libbed the famous line, "I'm king of the world!", which Jack shouts as he stands at the head of the ship.

APPLES, PEACHES, AND RASPBERRIES ARE ALL MEMBERS OF THE ROSE FAMILY.

CANADIAN RADIO STATIONS MUST PROMOTE CANADIAN MUSICIANS.

According to the Canadian Radio-Television and Telecommunications Commission, one out of every five songs played on the radio in Canada must be by a Canadian musician.

CROWS CAN REMEMBER
THE FACES OF INDIVIDUAL
HUMANS. THEY CAN ALSO
HOLD A GRUDGE.

ALL CLOWNFISH ARE BORN MALE.

All clownfish are born male. They have the ability to switch their sex, but will do so only to become the dominant female of a group.

FORTUNE TELLING IS ILLEGAL IN MARYLAND.

USING FERRETS TO HUNT OTHER ANIMALS IS ILLEGAL IN WEST VIRGINIA.

THERE ARE OVER 700 ANCIENT EGYPTIAN HIEROGLYPHIC SYMBOLS.

GREYHOUNDS CAN RUN UP TO 45 MPH.

BEES ARE THE ONLY INSECT THAT PRODUCE FOOD THAT PEOPLE EAT.

Honey is the only food made by an insect that humans eat. It is also interesting that honey found in the Egyptian pyramids was over 3,000 years old yet was still edible.

SOURCES

P4. https://www.ewboats.com/company/news/the-statue-of-liberty

P5. https://www.visitscotland.com/about/uniquely-scottish/national-animal-unicorn

P6. https://nypost.com/2020/05/13/why-its-illegal-to-own-only-one-guinea-pig-in-switzerland

P6. https://www.quora.com/Is-It-True-That-The-word-Pennsylvania-is-misspelled-on-the-Liberty-Bell

P8. https://www.toureiffel.paris/en/news/history-and-culture/why-does-eiffel-tower-change-size

P9. https://www.cookingchanneltv.com/devour/2013/09/germany-beer-pipeline

P9. https://factrepublic.com/facts/33802

P10. https://www.smithsonianmag.com/innovation/accidental-invention-bubble-wrap-180971325

P13. https://www.cdc.gov/mosquitoes/about/what-is-a-mosquito.html

P13. https://www.funfactsabout.net/20-interesting-cat-facts/

P14. https://www.akc.org/expert-advice/lifestyle/fun-facts-about-the-pembroke-welsh-corgi

P16. http://www.arizonapetvet.com/blog/can-certain-snails-really-sleep-for-3-years

P18. https://www.news18.com/news/lifestyle/did-you-know-men-were-the-first-to-wear-high-heel-shoes-2881163.html

P21. https://www.worldwideboat.com/news/miscellaneous/ocean-vs-space

P22. https://www.mvorganizing.org/how-do-we-measure-the-depth-of-the-sea

P25. https://www.houstonchronicle.com/news/nation-world/article/London-s-Big-Ben-leaning-a-little-2212087.php

P25. https://squareup.com/us/en/townsquare/the-history-of-the-dollar-bill

P26. https://rehabilitationrobotics.net/which-organ-in-the-digestive-tract-is-the-longest/

P27. https://www.washingtonpost.com/news/grade-point/wp/2015/01/14/brigham-young-university-adjusts-anti-beard-policies-amid-student-protests/

P29. https://www.forbes.com/sites/trevornace/2017/07/26/famous-easter-island-heads-have-hidden-bodies/?sh=76422bf1f804

P30. https://fortune.com/2015/10/01/gatorade-turns-50/

P31. https://nonickel.com/pages/harry-potters-daniel-radcliffe-has-nickel-allergy

P33. https://www.businessinsider.com/astronauts-avoid-burping-space-because-gravity-2018-11

P34. https://www.informationplanet.com/countries/australia

P35. https://www.feelingvegas.com/why-casinos-dont-have-clocks-windows

P36. https://www.snopes.com/fact-check/lincoln-wrestling-hall-of-fame

P37. https://ostritec.com/blog/the-ostrich-is-the-largest-bird-and-they-have-big-eyes-to-match

P38. https://www.facebook.com/ScienceEvidenceIntelligence/posts/metal-snow-at-the-very-top-of-venuss-mountains-beneath-the-thick-clouds-is-a-lay/905461236971252

P40. https://news.virginia.edu/content/presidential-fuming-7-historic-outbursts-jackson-obama

P41. https://www.highsnobiety.com/p/blue-ivy-carter-billboard-hot-100

P43. https://www.royal.uk/swans

P46. https://artsandculture.google.com/entity/m01ty_2?hl=es

P49. https://www.facebook.com/Joint.OPSEC.Support/posts/heres-a-little-trivia-for-everyone-did-you-know-that-at-one-point-the-penta-gon-a/1554470887905959

P49. https://www.thekitchn.com/the-tomato-has-more-genes-than-a-human-food-news-172066

P50. https://www.history.com/this-day-in-history/president-john-tyler-weds-his-second-wife

P50. https://www.atlasobscura.com/articles/theres-only-one-state-where-you-can-become-a-master-cheesemaker

P53. https://www.scientificamerican.com/article/is-it-true-that-hot-water

P53. https://www.goldmedalwineclub.com/blog/post/what-country-is-the-biggest-supplier-of-cork-243

P54. https://www.fs.usda.gov/detail/fishlake/home/?cid=STELPRDB5393641

P54. https://kids.kiddle.co/Hawaii_2

P56. https://clintonwhitehouse4.archives.gov/WH/glimpse/top.html

P57. https://www.foodnewsnews.com/news/how-to-tell-when-an-avocado-is-ripe-on-the-tree/

P58. https://simple.wikipedia.org/wiki/Tonic_immobility

P60. https://www.roadsideamerica.com/story/24951

P61. https://www.newscientist.com/question/many-hearts-octopus

P62. http://www.todayifoundout.com/index.php/2013/01/difference-between-kosher-salt-and-regular-salt/

P63. https://crazyfacts.com/charles-dickens-always-slept-facing-nort/

P64. https://www.mountvernon.org/the-estate-gardens/distillery/

P66. https://www.looper.com/210613/the-minions-language-in-despicable-me-explained/

P67. https://www.brainfutures.org/blog/top-brain-facts-august-2018/

P69. https://podcasts.google.com/feed/aHR0cHM6Ly9mZWVkcy5ucHIub3JnLzUxMDMxMy9wb2RjYXN0LnhtbA/episode/NjYxYWFmYTUtOTRiM-i00NGQ1LWE5MzEtYTMxODJhOWZkYTFl

P70. https://abcnews.go.com/Technology/facebook-relationship-status/story?id=16406245

P72. https://www.history.com/news/11-things-you-may-not-know-about-paul-revere

P74. https://swine.extension.org/is-it-true-that-pigs-do-not-have-sweat-glands-and-therefore-are-not-able-to-get-rid-of-toxins-in-their-bodies-i-e-mak-ing-the-pork-meat-unhealthy-to-eat

P74. https://www.thefiscaltimes.com/2015/09/21/Bouncer-Pope-21-Fascinating-Facts-About-Pope-Francis

P76. https://southfloridareporter.com/in-the-1600s-brandy-was-used-instead-of-mercury-in-thermometers

P78. https://en.wikipedia.org/wiki/Toto_(Oz)

P81. https://www.akc.org/expert-advice/news/remembering-dogs-titanic

P82. https://www.fearof.net/fear-of-opinions-phobia-allodoxaphobia

P83. https://www.usatoday.com/story/news/factcheck/2020/10/28/fact-check-9-things-women-couldnt-do-1971-mostly-right/3677101001

P84. https://www.loveexploring.com/gallerylist/69008/weird-laws-around-the-world

P85. https://blogs.scientificamerican.com/guest-blog/exploring-the-dromedairy-camels-and-their-milk

P86. https://www.livescience.com/33700-bulls-charge-red.html

P87. https://kybourbon.com/industry/impact

P88. https://en.wikipedia.org/wiki/Millie%27s_Book

P89. http://www.bio.utexas.edu/courses/evolution/crowneuks1.pdf

P89. https://www.boston.com/news/history/2015/07/02/this-womans-one-piece-bathing-suit-got-her-arrested-in-1907

P90. https://www.howitworksdaily.com/can-porcupines-float-on-water

P92. https://www.amusingplanet.com/2013/08/worlds-shortest-commercial-flight-is.html

P93. http://tonymusings.blogspot.com/2015/08/a-blessing-of-unicorns.html

P95. https://www.oklahoman.com/article/5622020/more-stars-than-grains-of-sand-on-earth-you-bet

P96. https://www.nigms.nih.gov/education/fact-sheets/Pages/circadian-rhythms.aspx

P97. http://didyouknowstuff.com/cucumber-can-actually-cure-bad-breath-a-slice-pressed-to-the-roof-of-your-mouth-for-30-seconds-with-your-tongue-allows-the-phytochemicals-to-kill-the-problematic-bacteria

P97. https://www.space.com/19116-astronauts-taller-space-spines.html

P98. https://www.thebalanceeveryday.com/why-have-skill-testing-questions-for-sweepstakes-896839

P98. https://scool.buzz/north-koreans-can-only-choose-a-hairstyle-from-30-state-approved-cuts

P101.https://parade.com/1019842/marynliles/weird-facts

P102.https://en.wikipedia.org/wiki/Bonobo

P103.https://www.nationalgeographic.com/animals/article/animals-sense-earthquakes

P105.https://sciencemadefun.net/blog/think-about-it-thursday-how-far-does-the-average-human-walk-in-a-lifetime

P105.https://www.bbc.com/news/science-environment-23410137

P106.https://metro.co.uk/2019/02/08/leonardo-dicaprio-didnt-want-say-iconic-im-king-world-titanic-shook-8482224

P107.https://crtc.gc.ca/eng/cancon/r_cdn.htm

P109.https://www.nationalgeographic.com/animals/fish/facts/clownfish#:~:text=Changing%20Sex,The%20change%20is%20irreversible.

P109.https://www.ontariohoney.ca/kids-zone/bee-facts